EQi 2.0 Study Guide

Strengthen Your Emotional Intelligence

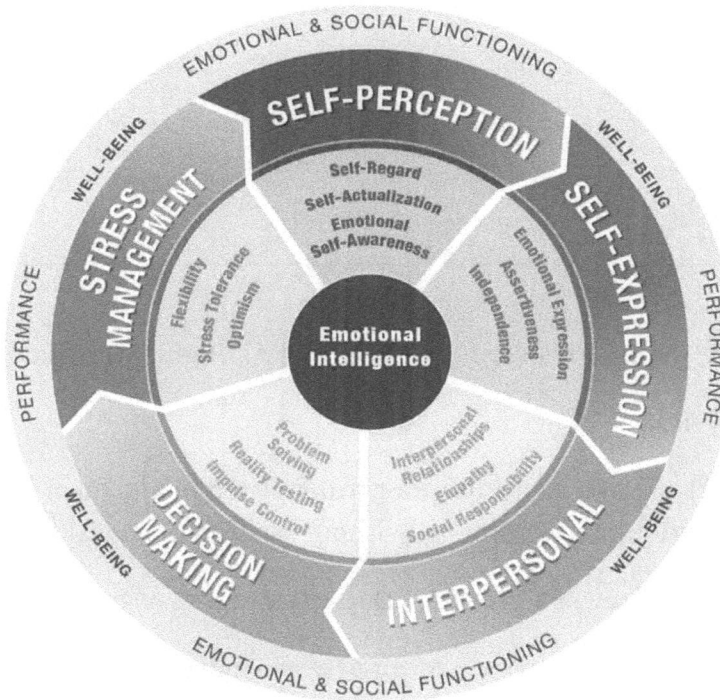

Cynthia Howard PhD, LSSBB

Emotional intelligence is your ability to be effective
when the pressure is on.

Cynthia Howard PhD, LSSBB

CONTENTS

OVERVIEW OF EI (EMOTIONAL INTELLIGENCE)

"We all have 'emotional intelligence'. We have to make the decision to engage it more often, to accomplish what we want."

Dr. Cynthia Howard

Emotional intelligence (EI) is the ability to identify and regulate your impulses, empathize with others, and persist in the face of pressure and obstacles. EI is a set of skills developed for a more remarkable ability to manage, lead, persuade, communicate, and perform.

These competencies, self-awareness, and self-management, are the foundation of high-performance leadership.

This diagram reflects the essential competencies of EI:

What am I feeling?

Why am I feeling it?

How do I use these emotions? (Action)

What happened? Evaluate the results.

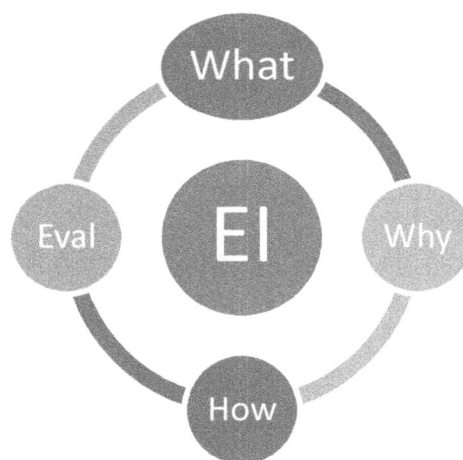

BARRIERS TO BETTER EI

Self-awareness is at the foundation of EI. Knowing what is going on within is critical so you can more deliberately respond to your environment. This section presents behavior that inhibits your EI. We all do these from time to time, some more than others. It is essential to learn how your resistance shows up.

The following are barriers to exercising a strong EI:

1. Under (or over) estimate yourself
2. Habit of negativity
3. Fail to commit or give 100%
4. Blame others
5. Not investing in yourself
6. Over (or under) reacting
7. Lack of introspection
8. Closed mind
9. Lack of curiosity
10. Status quo mindset ("I have always done it this way;" "This is just the way I am.")

When do these show up for you?

Write out an example of when you may have fallen into this trap in the last three days:

COACHABLE MINDSET

Being coachable is a valuable trait. It is

the willingness to learn and the desire to act.

Being willing to learn means you give up control and embrace what you do not know. It is the ability to take feedback and recognize you can learn a new way to improve. This is the first part of the equation. You must also be willing to act. What are you going to do about what you learned?

Emotional intelligence is one of the areas many leaders throw up resistance. For example, an executive may hear something about Empathy and say, "Yeah, yeah, I know I have to listen more..." and then tune out everything else, completely missing the more profound points around demonstrating Empathy or being present to people. And it impacts the bottom line!

Please keep an open mind as you go through this program. This program will upgrade your leadership, which will take you further ahead faster. I have had scores of leaders go through this; the proof is their success.

Being coachable means being open, curious, asking questions, and trying new behaviors. You have turned on your self-awareness and can begin to see how Ei may work for you.

The opposite is to resist anything new and show up for the training or sessions without any interest in understanding how this can work for you.

The self-actualization dimension of Ei is most closely related to this valuable characteristic. **Where did you score?**

We will be exploring it. Use this exercise to get honest with you and identify what you want to see differently in your leadership. Journal your thoughts on the next page.

YOUR GOAL FOR THIS COACHING EXPERIENCE

Think about those areas in which you want your leadership to improve. **What do you want to see differently for yourself? Write this out in measurable terms.**

Why do you want this? What will it do for you?

To be more successful, I will do

MORE	LESS

ACTION PLAN

Date	Skills Needed	Benefits	Support, Resources Needed	Potential Barriers

MY SCORES

Place a checkmark from your report in the LOW, MEDIUM, or HIGH range for that subscale score.

Fill in the right side of the table.

EQi 2.0 Results				
	LOW	MEDIUM	HIGH	
SELF-PERCEPTION				Describe current role:
Self-Regard				
Self-Actualization				
Self-Awareness				
SELF-EXPRESSION				
Emotional Expression				
Assertiveness				
Independence				
INTERPERSONAL				**3 GOALS**
Relationships				
Empathy				These are three goals you have for your professional career this year.
Social Responsibility				
DECISION-MAKING				1.
Problem-Solving				
Reality Testing				2.
Impulse Control				
STRESS MANAGEMENT				3.
Flexibility				
Stress Tolerance				
Optimism				
WELL-BEING				
Happiness				

To help you focus your development goals, look at your three highest and lowest scores. Write them in the table below.

Highest Scales	Lowest Scales

This guidebook details each dimension, including what happens when you overdo that scale. That section is *EQi Subscales in Detail.*

Before you get there, take 7 minutes and reflect on the following questions. Review each subscale and consider the following:

Am I happy with where I am on this subscale?

What success stories can I talk about regarding this subscale?

When did I underperform on this subscale, and what were the circumstances?

If I were to ask a trusted friend, in what areas would they say I OVER or UNDER perform as a leader?

EQi 2.0: Making Sense of the Score

The EQi 2.0 is a powerful tool because it opens you up to learning more about yourself. This is where the tool's power lies – in developing self-awareness. This self-awareness translates into personal power.

Too often, the quick overview of the score leaves people with a "good or bad" impression of their emotional intelligence. This is an oversimplification. The score is only part of the story.

Look at the continuum of scores. **Keep in mind the goal of this process is to increase your self-awareness, not to be perfect.**

Low				High
Low engagement. Low skills.	Overly selective about using emotional skills.	50% of respondents fall in this category. Room for growth. Inconsistent engagement.	High engagement and developed skills could have overdone strengths.	Overdone strengths likely. Arrogance Perfectionism Blind to reality

We all have some degree of emotional intelligence. Most people need to choose to engage in it more often. This can be due to a lack of skills in specific areas:

- Conflict competence
- Problem-solving
- Decision making
- Self-care (stress management)
- Emotional awareness
- Active listening

LEADERSHIP POTENTIAL

The EQi 2.0 and the subscales indicate leadership competencies that increase productivity and decrease employee turnover while boosting efficiency.

Leaders who engage the competencies in these four areas are more likely to increase work satisfaction, create trust, and foster organizational commitment and loyalty.

You should focus your development on these areas.

Leadership Strengths Chart

Authenticity		Insight	
Self-actualization		Self-Actualization	
Reality Testing		Optimism	
Self-Regard		Self-Regard	
Emotional Self Awareness		Social responsibility	
Social Responsibility		Interpersonal relationships	
Independence		Emotional Expression	
Innovation		**Coaching**	
Self-actualization		Self-actualization	
Independence		Empathy	
Problem-Solving		Reality testing	
Assertiveness		Interpersonal relationships	
Flexibility		Assertiveness	
Optimism		Emotional self-awareness	

Write in your scores for these dimensions.

Leadership Derailers or Blind Spots

The four scales below have the potential to derail your influence. Write in your scores.

Impulse Control	
Stress Tolerance	
Problem-Solving	
Independence	

What competencies are your strongest?

What skills do you most need now in your current role?

What strategies will you implement to mitigate the derailers?

QUESTIONS FOR EACH LEADERSHIP COMPETENCY

The following questions will help you identify what practices and daily activities help you demonstrate any of the leadership styles. Write out your thoughts below each question.

Authenticity

Authenticity in a leader commands confidence from their transparency and fairness. Why do you think authenticity is an essential component of leadership?

How do you demonstrate authenticity?

Insight

A leader provides insight by sharing a purpose and a vision for colleagues to follow. This encourages employees to exceed goals. How do you encourage your staff?

Innovation

Being innovative is not just about solving problems but how one takes advantage of opportunities and engages everyone in the process of positive change.

How are you fostering innovation through your leadership?

In what ways do you promote an innovative culture?

Coaching

When leaders coach their staff, they are seen as nurturing and supportive, helping individuals grow and stretch themselves.

How does a leader know when they are being a coach?

What specific observable behaviors and actions are associated with coaching?

EQi Subscales in Detail

In this section, you have more details on the 16 dimensions of the EQi 2.0. As you read through your EQi 2.0 report, you may focus on specific dimensions more than others. At some point, review all the dimensions to understand better how you can strengthen your ability to perform well under pressure.

The goal of strengthening your emotional intelligence (EI) is not to "perfect" these skills but rather to be flexible and adaptable as the situation demands.

Too often, emotional intelligence is considered a scorecard - high scores are excellent, and low scores are bad. This approach is a gross oversimplification behind Ei, missing out on meaningful development opportunities. Effective Ei means you have and know how to balance these different and sometimes conflicting behaviors.

There are four ways to overdo a strength:

1. Frequency – behavior is relied upon, used too often, and becomes repetitive and predictable.

2. Intensity – too much emphasis on or passion behind the behavior.

3. Duration – behavior engaged for too long becomes tedious and loses its effect.

4. Context - behavior is the wrong tool/approach for a given time or situation.

Self-Perception

- Self-regard
- Self-Actualization
- Emotional Self Awareness

Self-Expression

- Emotional Expression
- Assertiveness
- Independence

- Relationships
- Empathy
- Social responsibility

Decision making

- Problem-Solving
- Reality Testing
- Impulse Control

Stress Management

- Flexibility
- Stress Tolerance
- Optimism

We describe each dimension, ways you may be overdoing it, and suggestions to be more effective.

SELF-REGARD

This is one of the most challenging scales to grasp. It may be because most professionals are geared toward focusing on their weaknesses rather than entirely on their true strengths. A lot of mental and physical energy is freed up when you are confident in your ability. Being self-assured allows you to focus on what is required of you at the moment rather than getting sidetracked by personal interactions that may create insecurity or conflict. Instead of stewing or ruminating about the interaction, with confidence in yourself, you can assess your part in it, take the action that will best serve the ultimate goal, and move on. You do not need to be defensive.

You will grow and develop stronger self-regard as you interact, reflect on these interactions, and make corrections.

This dimension is your ability to own your strengths, accept your weaknesses, and feel confident and self-assured.

Do your actions reflect this inner belief in yourself, or are you seeking validation, approval, and support from others?

With intense self-regard, you:

- Express your ideas and thoughts confidently and be comfortable in the process
- Pursue your goals and be sensitive to others
- Accepts compliments graciously
- Asks for help when needed and responds when asked

What gets in the way:

- Self-assessment that is weighted toward weaknesses
- Perfectionism
- Lack of time to reflect

✍ Journal. Start your Success List. Review regularly.

Overdone Self Regard

Overdone Self-Regard can be a debilitating problem. Excessive Self-Regard tends to yield feedback that you are:

- Arrogant
- Vain and conceited
- Narcissistic
- Over-confident
- Superior to others

Fall out in Personal Relationships

Personal relationships can suffer when overdone. Self-Regard shows up as arrogance and narcissism. The attention demanded and expected by the over-sized ego is at odds with any partnership. The more overdone Self-Regard is, the harder it will be to set personal needs aside to focus on the other.

Fall out in Leadership

Self-confidence is not only attractive in a leader but also essential. However, leaders can be repellant when that self-confidence crosses the line into arrogance and an air of superiority. Leaders who rely on their relationships to influence may find that overdoing Self-Regard can create a toxic effect.

Team and Organizational Expressions

Teams and Organizations with over-engaged Self-Regard tend to be entitled, held up with arrogance, and almost invincible. The expectation is that they will win or succeed because they deserve it. This collective over-indulgence in Self-Regard usually closes their eyes to flaws and vulnerabilities and steers them away from receiving criticism or feedback. This becomes a vicious cycle.

Suggested Actions to Balance Self-Regard:

Suppose you over-engage (in frequency, intensity, duration, and context) Self-Regard. In that case, the solution is not to like yourself less (to be timid or uncertain) but to balance those tendencies that drive you toward excessive Self-Regard.

1. Stop in and talk to people. Spend time and demonstrate concern for them, their interests, and their lives. Keep a spreadsheet with these details to help you remember in future conversations. Active listening will help you build trust.

2. Offer tokens of appreciation and gifts to let people know you were thinking of them. This does not have to be expensive; small gestures are appreciated.

3. Open up and share more about you. It could be one of the goals you had but missed or a disappointment. Sharing at the right time can make you seem more approachable and "human."

If Self-Regard is low:

1. Compliment yourself. Use positive statements when describing yourself. Watch your self-talk.

2. Offer opinions so people get to know you.

3. Tune into body language; sit up straight, put your shoulders back, make eye contact, and smile.

SELF-ACTUALIZATION (COACH-ABILITY)

This is your ability to pursue meaningful goals and become the very best you can be. This means you have met your primary needs and are ready to pursue what brings you joy and meaning. This characteristic is reflected in your ability to be honest with yourself, your motives, and your values. This honesty contributes to confidence, comfort in being with others, openness, lack of judgment and prejudice, and a passion for life.

This dimension demonstrates:

- Autonomy
- Energy in pursuit of goals
- Spontaneity
- Enthusiasm
- Willingness to grow, learn, take action

What gets in the way:

- Focus on status and external motivation
- Lack of personal values
- Fear of failure
- Loss of motivation, drive
- Victim identity
- Blaming others

⌖ Review your goals. Are you focused on programs that will move you closer to your goals?

Self-Regard, Self-Actualization & Optimism: Power Blend

Check your scores in these three areas. Remember that high scores do not necessarily mean "good," and low scores mean "bad;" instead, the balance among the scores is most significant. Write down your scores:

Self-Regard	Self-Actualization	Optimism

What area is out of balance?

Power Blend Reflection:

Self-Regard

Tendency to accept and like yourself in full view of positive and negative qualities. Confident despite perceived weaknesses. Focus is on what one can do vs barriers to success.

What will you do to balance this area:

Self-Actualization (Coach-ability)

Your ability to grow, see potential, be willing to learn new things, and act. Reflects honesty with Self and an ability to set goals and pursue them.

What will you do to balance this area:

Optimism

Your ability to see the positive despite challenges. Your view of the future is hopeful. This dimension reflects your confidence in your ability to focus.

What will you do to balance this area:

Overdone Self Actualization

Overdone Self-Actualization can be a debilitating problem. Do you tend to be:

- Perpetually dissatisfied with the status quo
- Overly goal-driven—too intense
- Overly exuberant with your activities and points of passion
- Self-centered--blind to the needs and interests of others
- Unwilling to do tasks that are not personally enriching

Fall out in Personal Relationships

In a relationship, too much Self-Actualization manifests as a drive to strive and achieve, whereas many relationships require love, support, and nurturance instead—these are not always compatible energies. "Be with me—don't try to fix me." "Take comfort in our relationship—don't see it as a growth opportunity or a challenge course."

Fall out in Leadership

Leaders who overdose on Self-Actualization tend to wring out and exhaust those who follow them with perpetual striving and raising the bar. No output or level of performance is ever quite good enough. Borders are overly ambitious, whose approval or attention tends to be earned with displays of hard work and struggle.

Team and Organizational Expressions

When a team or organization over-engages in this self-actualization, the culture demands constant improvement but never actually gets "there."

Suggestions:

1. Acknowledge the gap between your expectations for achievement and those of your team, boss, and coworkers. Consider the impact on your team of your added striving and how it will yield added achievement – or not.

2. Select a set goal and consider at least two more relaxed outcomes you could work toward and be satisfied with. If this kind of brainstorming is difficult for you to do on your own, conduct a brainstorming session with a colleague or workgroup to generate at least two other options—this is designed to increase your Flexibility, not lower the bar or settle for mediocrity

EMOTIONAL SELF AWARENESS

This is the foundation of emotional intelligence. When you know what is going on inside, what motivates you, what triggers you, and what you feel – you can act intentionally and in line with your goals. When you are out of touch with yourself, you may come off as a "loose cannon," "a bull in a china shop," out of touch or clueless. Do you overestimate your abilities or your weaknesses? Are you blind to your growing edge?

To develop yourself further, you must know where you are now. This awareness extends to your impact on others and keeps you open to receiving feedback. As you increase your understanding of yourself, you also increase your awareness of others; you listen better, are more comfortable with conflict, and can coach others.

Self-awareness is reflected in:

- Self-acceptance
- Self-understanding
- Effective emotional expression
- Ability to accept feedback

What gets in the way:

- Low Empathy
- Self-centeredness
- Competitiveness

The following is an inventory and self-check on significant emotions. Are you avoiding some feelings? Evaluate yourself...

Self-Awareness: Emotional Fitness

Most people go through their day locked into a habitual pattern of reacting. Only when you begin to question your reactions/ emotions do you begin to understand what you are feeling and why.

Take a moment and reflect on the history of your emotional patterns; in reflecting, you can break through any patterns that no longer work for you.

What have your role models taught you about emotions?

How well do you identify and manage your emotions on a scale from 1 to 10? One is Not Usually. Ten is Very well and Consistently.

1_____5_____10

Explain:

Emotional Awareness Exercise

The more aware you are of what is happening within you, the more you can manage what is happening around you. Most people live in a habitual pattern of responses.

This exercise helps you clarify your patterns. This is an excellent introduction to your emotions. These exercises build self-awareness, a hallmark of a successful leader.

To help you tune in and become more aware of your emotional experience, evaluate the following questions:

Anger ❤ Happiness ❤ Anxiety ❤ Fear ❤ Sadness

1.	What feeling is usually most intense for you using a 1-10 scale?

	0 ——————————————————————————— 10

2.	What feeling is most frequent on a 1- 10 scale?

	0 ——————————————————————————— 10

3.	What people or situations trigger this feeling?

4.	What is the typical outcome because of this emotion? Does it impact your relationships, job, energy levels, or motivation?

Overdone Self Awareness

Excessive Emotional Self-Awareness tends to yield feedback that you are:

- Self-consumed—seeing things unrelated to you only through your emotional filters
- Self-centered
- Self-indulgent
- Insensitive to the needs and concerns of others

Relationship Fall out

In a relationship, too much Emotional Self-Awareness comes across as selfish and self-consumed. Everything in the relationship (even things happening to and with the other person) triggers self-focused thoughts. With too much Emotional Self-Awareness in a relationship, time can be spent overly analyzing the nuance of emotional changes rather than engaging with your partner.

Leadership Fall out

The self-focused attention of excessive Emotional Self-Awareness can pull a leader into himself, distracting him from engaging the people and tasks he's charged to lead.

Team and Organizational Expressions

The irony of teams and organizations with over-engaged Emotional Self-Awareness is that there is a cultural value in prizing self-awareness and a rich vocabulary of emotions and their shades of difference. Yet, despite all this identification and consideration, there needs to be more engagement. **A byproduct of excessive Emotional Self-awareness can be a tendency to reflect more than engage.**

Suggestions to balance Excessive Self Awareness

One of the most significant ways to show connection and concern for other people is to express curiosity about them—ask them what they are feeling and pay attention to their reply.

- When in discussion with someone, go beyond listening to their actual words and pay attention to their non-verbal communication to see what emotional cues they hold:

    - Eye contact (eye to eye or eyes averted)

    - Gestures (nervous, fidgety, open)

    - Posture (open, blocked, facing you, turned away)

    - Tone of Voice (loud and aggressive, fearful, quiet and timid) (This is using Empathy to balance Emotional Self-Awareness)

- Find one group or cause, local or global--and commit to helping them with one project or effort.
- Verify your perceptions. Ask at least two other people to describe an event you shared or experienced together, noting the details common to all accounts.

♥

Anybody can become angry - that is easy,

but to be angry with the right *person and*

to the right *degree and at the* right *time and*

for the proper purpose and in the right *way -*

that is not within everybody's power and is not easy.

- Aristotle, born 384 BC

EMOTIONAL SELF EXPRESSION

This skill set is best described by Aristotle's quote on the previous page. Do you express your emotions directly and appropriately with intensity, thoughtfulness, respect, and clarity?

Emotions are often thought of as the enemy, unpredictable and or unnecessary. Yet, they are built into our nervous system and required to make decisions. Antonio Damasio, MD, and neuroscientist writes in *Self Comes to Mind* that emotions are automatic, programmed into our nervous system, and without them, decisions are impossible.

❧ Fact: First, we feel, then we think. ❧

EI's 'emotional expression' dimension is your ability to be in touch with and express what is happening within you. While emotions may be impacted by what is happening around you, emotions are based on your interpretation of what is happening around you. It is your perspective that is significant and not what is happening.

Emotions happen. What you can control is your expression of them. Research has found that naming an emotion improves your ability to express it. An exercise in the "awareness" section will help you tune into basic emotions and build your vocabulary.

On the next page is a list of feeling words. Please read through them, make a note of those you use often, and find words that better describe what you think. This is a process and takes practice. The better your vocabulary, the better you are at expressing yourself.

Strong Emotional Expression:

- You identify what you feel and express it at the right time
- Recognize that emotions are simply part of you, and it is the timing and tone of expression that causes the problem
- Able to express a wide range of emotions

What gets in the way:

- Lack of self-awareness
- Lack of role models for healthy expression
- Cultural bias toward emotional expression
- No practice

Emotional Vocabulary

Emotions happen and, ideally, are not good or bad. They are warning lights on your dashboard. I have listed words here to help you identify what you are feeling. The more you can **name it - the more you can claim it,** giving you more control and confidence. This ultimately delays your reaction to your emotions.

Angry	Determined	Fulfilled	Joyful
Affectionate	Delighted	Gregarious	Jealous
Adequate	Distant	Grateful	Lonely
Annoyed	Distraught	Glad	Loved
Anxious	Dubious	Guilty	Mad
Betrayed	Defeated	Happy	Miserable
Bitter	Eager	Hopeful	Overwhelmed
Bored	Energized	Honored	Overjoyed
Bodacious	Excited	Hardy	Panicked
Calm	Empty	Hopeless	Perplexed
Capable	Envious	Helpless	Peaceful
Challenged	Fatigued	Inspired	Pleased
Cheerful	Frustrated	Impressed	Proud
Confused	Foolish	Intimidated	Relieved
Content	Friendly	Irritated	Refreshed
Relaxed	Satisfied	Unsettled	
Safe	Threatened	Vulnerable	
Sad	Trapped	Ashamed	

❧ Do you have trouble expressing yourself?

Here are a few tips.

If you start the interaction with:

You made me feel...

This can be a hot button for the person you are talking to and shut down the conversation. While your feelings may seem like someone's action triggers them, your feelings are *your* responsibility. It is powerful (and essential) for you to OWN your feelings.

Use this formula to express your feelings:

When this happened _____ (or you did or said,

I felt.

This approach will engage the other person rather than putting them off with "*You made me feel*" as they experience this as you are blaming them. Now, you have the chance to dialogue and understand each other. This also requires you to name your feelings, accept them as your responsibility, and take charge of them. This is empowering!

Do you explode or hold in your anger only to regret it later?

Use tapping, visualization, or resilience tools to unhook from the emotional charge and open your perspective.

❧ *Engage your senses—practice mindfulness.*

Overdone Emotional Expression

Excessive Emotional Expression tends to yield feedback that you are:

- Injecting yourself or your emotional state into issues non-related to you
- Emotionally transparent
- I am emotionally hijacking--making objective issues and events reasons to share personal data.
- Self-centered and self-indulgent

Relationship Fall out

Too much Emotional Expression can complicate and crowd a relationship by having the more emotional partner's feelings and emotional states dominate the relationship. Excessive Emotional Expression can also increase the expectations of the more emotionally expressive partner. There can be a belief that true love and connection are measured in the frequency and intensity of their expression, thus setting up disappointment when those emotional expressions are not reciprocated to that degree.

Leadership Fall out

Volatile and often exhausting to those who follow, the leader who overdoes Emotional Expression tends to display raw emotions using more dramatic words and emotional intensity. This can obscure the leader's authenticity.

Team and Organizational Expressions

Teams and Organizations with over-engaged Emotional Expression tend to share stories expecting visible reactions, a gasp, or grimace. Teams that collectively overdo Emotional Expression can fall into a top-me cycle in which the loudest, boldest, or most dramatic expression is engaged. They can miss out on solving issues and focusing on the most critical tasks.

Suggestions for Excessive Use of Emotional Expression:

Practice telling a story or recounting an event without exaggerating details, sticking to specific, verifiable facts. (This uses reality testing to balance emotional expression).

- Verify your perceptions and emotions. Ask at least two other people to describe an event you all shared or experienced together, noting the details and emotional words they use.

- In key meetings, reframe the highly charged emotional descriptors with moderate expressions: devastated becomes disappointed, ecstatic becomes happy.

ASSERTIVENESS

This dimension of emotional intelligence reminds me of Goldilocks and the 3 Bears; aggressive communication is way too much; passive is not enough, with Assertiveness being "just right."

Assertiveness is a communication style and one that takes practice. As you develop the other dimensions of EI, especially emotional expression and Independence, you will also be working on Assertiveness. In my master's thesis, I studied Assertiveness and its moderating influence on burnout – a significant skill. It did reduce the amount of stress a person experienced, reducing the incidence of burnout.

Assertiveness does not have good role models, so many need to learn what it looks like. The other problem is that in particular work and family cultures, speaking up is not valued, and the one speaking out can be ridiculed and shamed.

Don't rock the boat.

If it isn't broke don't fix it.

Who do you think you are?

Better to keep quiet...

If you speak up, you will be labeled bossy.

Women do not speak up.

I do not have the authority.

What if they do not like what I have to say?

Do you believe any of these? Have you heard them in your workplace or family? Part of activating your resilience and strengthening your emotional intelligence is to explore your beliefs and get rid of those that no longer serve you. Many people have trouble being assertive because they believe it is not part of their identity.

Assertiveness is respectful, intentional, and sensitive, and it means you set limits and boundaries and state your position clearly and evenly. Too often, people get angry and "assert" themselves only to come off as aggressive. Anger is one of the emotions that is feared and avoided. Unfortunately, you are then at risk of being hijacked by it and exploding. The message anger wants you to know is to set better boundaries!

Tips to stop the vicious cycle

Here are a few suggestions to stop the cycle of saying too much and then retreating and saying too little. Here is how you can get it "just right."

1. Start by taking small steps to speak up. Maybe you start in your social life, and instead of saying, "It doesn't matter," state your preference, "I want to go to this restaurant or movie." You will build confidence.

2. Set limits when you start to feel angry, resentful, or put upon. Say, "No," or "I will get back to you," or "I will think about it." This takes you out of the equation and allows you to see if this request aligns with your goals.

3. Practice active listening. Use your Card deck and review that. Be completely present when you listen to someone rather than thinking of an answer. This will help you to understand better what is being said and not said. Ask, "What is this person saying, and what do they want?" This enables you to know where that person is coming from so that you can decide how you want to handle the situation. *Believe it or not, listening can be an assertive action!*

4. Be sure to have the facts and keep your comments based on facts rather than personality. If you are problem-solving at work and have an aggressive person who attacks you, ignore the remark and redirect the person, "*This isn't about me. Let's focus on the situation.*"

    This is being assertive and maintaining control of the meeting and or interaction. This is a boundary you are setting. Keep the focus by looking at both sides of the issue – Pros and Cons. This is also important in Problem Solving and Decision Making – staying focused on finding the best solution rather than being reactive and taking the first best solution that may be the easiest but not the best.

5. Get feedback. Ask trusted friends or your mentor what they thought when you spoke up. Make Assertiveness a priority in your professional development.

6. **Use your Success Journal**. Doing the exercises and learning from your reflections will help you fine-tune when and how you speak up.

Think about a time when you were assertive. What was it like?

Identify a time when you were passive. How was it different?

Identify a time when you were aggressive. How is it different from being assertive?

What gets in the way:

- The belief that no one cares what you think
- Fear of rejection
- Lack of attention to being assertive
- Not taking feedback
- Not knowing "how" or "when" to be assertive

This skill takes practice. It will not serve you to "wait until" the right time to learn to speak up. Start now!

&⚫ Developing a comfort with being assertive will help you maintain balance so you can have energy left over for yourself!

Overdone Assertiveness

Excessive Assertiveness tends to yield feedback that you are:

- Aggressive
- Abusive
- Militant or even bossy
- Self-centered (commanding the spotlight and disproportionate airtime)

Relationship Fall out

The opinionated, aggressive, and even bullying behaviors that result from excessive Assertiveness can be toxic to a personal relationship. Winning becomes the goal at the expense of relating. There can be overuse of criticism in the name of clarity.

Leadership Fall out

Directive and bossy, the overly assertive leader will quickly compete, control, and criticize. Unfortunately, this can be common in hierarchical organizations, with a "my way or the highway" approach on most issues and decisions.

Team and Organizational Expressions

Teams and Organizations with over-engaged Assertiveness can forgo politeness and social courtesy in the name of winning.   The ends justify the means when unbalanced Assertiveness drives the culture.

Suggestions for Excessive Assertive:

Consider at least two other positions or points of view on an issue where your opinion is fixed. If this kind of brainstorming is difficult for you to do on your own, conduct a brainstorming session with a colleague or workgroup to generate at least two other options for a problem, conflict, or issue. This will generate new data for you to consider and position you as the facilitator of this change.

Practice Empathy.

INDEPENDENCE

Naturally, Independence follows Assertiveness. Being effective as a leader means you can navigate these competencies to collaborate and lead your team. Independence implies something other than being able to do your own thing. It means you can work, think, and act on your own, and you can also be a team member when needed.

> ❧ Your ability to adapt is significant and the most understated competency in EI. Independence is the competency to help you adjust.

Being independent means you do not rely on what other people think, can make decisions, and can take action when needed. When you have developed your Independence, you accept responsibility for your actions and decisions, get challenges, and take credit for your successes. You know that collaboration is critical to successful implementation.

This competency requires listening, setting boundaries, and having self-confidence. Too much Independence can make you look indifferent or aloof, and you end up feeling isolated, while too little can put you in a passive position and make you feel like a doormat.

What gets in the way:

- Negative self-talk
- Dependence on other opinions
- Lack of self-confidence
- Desire to fit in even at the expense of your own identity
- Experience of bullying and or put-downs
- A culture that does not value independent thoughts or innovation

TIPS

Do you find yourself doing the following?

- Refuse to ask for help? You can overdo the independence skill set! Ask for help; it can be a great way to collaborate.

- Do you hold back in hopes someone else will make the decision? If you rely on others to make the tough decision, it is time for you to step up to your leadership responsibility. Not deciding is deciding by default. This usually does not end up serving your team. They lose respect, and you lose power and confidence.

- Do you shop for advice? This can infuriate others who might feel you are discounting their offer to help. Develop the confidence to figure this out or to know who and when to ask for help.

- Do you critique everything you do and hesitate on what to do? Overthinking what you did wrong is the same as only looking at what you did well. It would help if you had a balanced perspective.

- When challenged, do you freeze up? This is a triggered reaction to stress. Remember to breathe and reset your stress set point. Practice active listening. What is the person asking and or concerned about? More than likely, it is a need for clarification and not necessarily a direct challenge. Either way, seek to clarify, not defend your position.

Assertiveness & Independence Balance

There is a natural tension between these two dimensions. Check your scores and take note of where you fall in this area.

A healthy balance between these dimensions will improve your influence and trust-building with your followers.

Related dimensions to consider:

- **Impulse control** (the more significant your impulse control, the less this dynamic will show up)
- Relationships

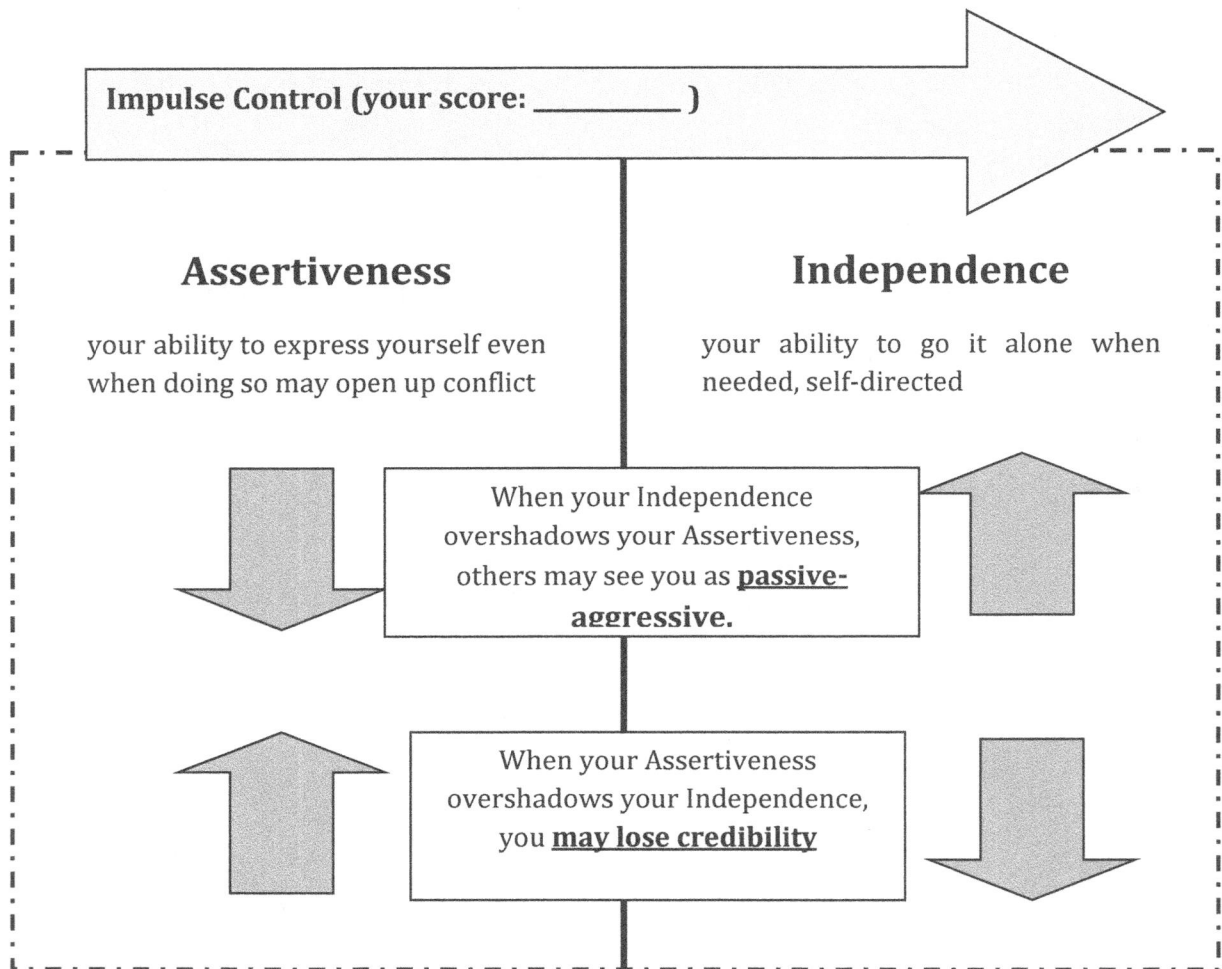

Impulse Control (your score: _____)

Assertiveness

your ability to express yourself even when doing so may open up conflict

Independence

your ability to go it alone when needed, self-directed

When your Independence overshadows your Assertiveness, others may see you as **passive-aggressive.**

When your Assertiveness overshadows your Independence, you **may lose credibility**

Assertiveness

Your ability to express yourself even when doing so may open up conflict.

What will you do to balance this area:

Independence

Your ability to go it alone when needed, self-directed.

What will you do to balance this area:

Impulse control

You can delay or filter an action to achieve the desired outcome.

What will you do to balance this area:

Overdone Independence

Excessive Independence tends to yield feedback that you are:

- Emotionally withholding
- Detached and un-collaborative
- Isolated
- Counter-dependent (you need authority to have something to push against)

Relationship Fall out

Overdone Independence is a force constantly pulling one out of a relationship. Most personal relationships develop and strengthen through an exchange of interests and interdependence. Excessive Independence leads to only one foot in (and, therefore, one foot out) of any relationship.

Leadership Fall out

Leaders overly engaged with Independence have succeeded because of their competent performance or expertise. They tend to over-rely on their competence and Independence to exclude interpersonal connection and engagement with others.

Team and Organizational Expressions

Teams and organizations with over-engaged Independence tend to disregard and minimize the importance of teams (and even meetings). Trust is not expected or given, and communication is on a "need-to-know" basis. Such hyper-independent workplaces can come across as a collection of individuals who work as a group.

Suggestion for Excessive Independence

Excessive Independence can lead to avoiding engagement and interaction and, therefore, avoidance of conflict and problem-solving. Consider the impact of not acting or solving any given issue or problem. If avoidance or inaction is postponement of the issue, isn't it easier to take some action? This is using Problem-Solving to balance Independence.

RELATIONSHIPS

Relationships are everything. We have relationships with coworkers, family, friends, ourselves, food, God, money, and so on. The most important relationship is the one you have with yourself. I hope this process of assessment and reflection has increased your self-acceptance and appreciation for yourself. It will help you develop better relationships with others.

This competency in EI is your ability to work with people to get the job done.

This is the goldmine of leadership competencies and will be enhanced as you develop the other skill sets. The ability to relate to others requires other skill sets in order to be effective. Just as no one wants to work with someone chronically negative, no one wants to work with someone overly social, constantly distracting, and not contributing to the overall workload.

As with all the competencies, success in this skill set requires balance. Awareness of how you are impacting others is central to a strong EI and allows you to self-correct and adjust your behavior to make the situation work.

> ം Question: Can you relate to all types of people, even those you may disagree with, to accomplish your mission?

Tips for Working Well Together

- Identify common ground
- Demonstrate interest in working together
- Spend time with the team
- Communicate directly and respectfully so everyone understands what is expected.
- Focus first on building trust and rapport, then focus on the tasks
- Practice active listening
- Handle conflict directly and respectfully vs. ignore defensive people and comments.
- Set up expectations for the projects.

What gets in the way:

- Lack of confidence
- Too much confidence and disinterest in collaborating with others
- Judgment/ prejudice
- Lack of familiarity with certain people
- Overly concerned with maintaining control
- Perfectionism, overly critical
- Disorganized and always in a rush

What are your observations about work relationships:

Overdone Relationships

Excessive Interpersonal Relationship tends to yield feedback that you are:

- Inappropriately familiar or intimate
- Too free or disclosing with personal data
- Too demanding or expectant of disclosure from others
- Co-dependent
- Unable or unwilling to be alone

Relationship Fall out

In a relationship, excessive use of this dimension can leave you appearing as emotionally volatile and smothering, with many demands or expectations to share, disclose, and connect and frequently (if not constantly) re-affirm that connection.

Leadership Fall out

Leaders with excessive Interpersonal Relationships overplay the relationship power base, believing those who follow them will do so primarily because of their relational connection *and affection* for the leader. Guilt can often be a leverage point for this leader, who avoids feedback due to the conflict or clash that might arise. This can leave followers needing clarification and support.

Team and Organizational Expressions

Teams and Organizations with over-engaged Interpersonal Relationships tend to be conflict-avoidant, often placing group harmony, interpersonal connection, and group cohesion more critical than task completion, the bottom line, or other more objective measures of progress of success. These hyper-sensitive systems tend, therefore, to avoid criticism and feedback and can, as a result, be slow to learn and reluctant to move beyond their comfort zone.

Suggestions for Excessive Relationships

Explore the uniqueness of your personality with strengths-based profiles or the Myers Briggs. Coaching is helpful to develop a deeper understanding of your value contributions, decreasing your dependence on others.

- Get a hobby or activity you pursue alone.
- Take the initiative to assume responsibility and accountability for a project--or even a tiny piece of one--agreeing to get it done yourself.

EMPATHY

We all like and need recognition; to be understood, seen, valued, and acknowledged is at the core of Empathy. Leaders need to demonstrate Empathy, yet there is little "education and training" on how to show Empathy effectively. It is expected to come naturally. Yet, the stressors typical in the day-to-day activity of leading and managing can disconnect one from their ability to be present, authentic, and actively engaged with staff. These distractions during the day interfere with the healthy expression of Empathy.

Empathy is often confused with sympathy and over-caring. Over-identifying with the "Caregiver" role gets in the way of Empathy; instead, "rescuing" takes place, draining the person who is doing the rescuing and not empowering the person who is being rescued.

As a leader, demonstrating Empathy can become even more challenging in the name of "getting things done" and being accountable. This training will help you balance "relationships and results" in your day-to-day leadership.

By shining the light on emotional awareness and diving into the intelligence of emotions, learning more about Empathy will help you add structure to 'it,' enabling you to better demonstrate your connection and understanding with others.

A simplified definition of Empathy:

> *Empathy is a set of emotional and behavioral skills that allows one to connect with, understand, and relate to another to provide support.*

Empathy and the understanding of it are evolving. The word itself was only coined in 1909! It was used to describe a cognition (thought) and a visceral (gut) experience in understanding art and aesthetics.

Empathy and sympathy were considered synonyms; today, they are more opposites. Today, as more is understood about Empathy, it is not enough to relate to the emotions of others. Instead, it is also essential to take action to understand their feelings. This can only happen if you relate well to your own emotions.

Here is where your EI strength will help you better express Empathy.

Reflection

Are you effective in expressing your emotions and or acknowledging them in others?

Are you "generous" in your ability to listen?

Do you feel drained by other people's emotions? (This could indicate you are close to burnout or experiencing compassion fatigue. What do you have to do to take care of yourself?)

Do you get caught in the trap of caretaking others?

Overdone Empathy

Excessive Empathy tends to yield feedback that you are:

- Emotionally dependent
- Unable or unwilling to differentiate yourself and your emotional needs from others'
- Dishonest, which can mean holding back the truth when it may hurt
- Conflict avoidant
- Overly attached to others, can be overwhelmed by others' emotions that you can't function

Relationship Fall out

In a relationship, too much Empathy leads to an emotional dependency and getting lost in your partner's emotions. He is sad, so you are. Identity can be lost while you become the relationship's moving receiver and radio tower.

Leadership Fall out

Leaders with an excess of Empathy are so curious about and concerned for those they lead that they shrink from making decisions that will hurt feelings and bruise relationships. A hyper-focus on people and their feelings can distract a leader from more objective issues and problems, making the leader appear weak, overly personal, or indecisive.

Team and Organizational Expressions

Teams and Organizations with over-engaged Empathy tend to have and promote values of selflessness. An individual's identity, and therefore his success within this culture, is defined by how much attention he can pay to clients and patients. This can lead to groupthink or mediocre performance because no one wants to step outside the group.

Suggestions for Excessive Empathy

Become curious about your mood and feelings. Check-in with you throughout your day and increase your awareness of your thoughts and feelings. If writing appeals to you, keep a journal and note how you feel to connect your thoughts, behaviors, and emotions. Use Emotional Self-awareness to balance Empathy.

SOCIAL RESPONSIBILITY

This dimension of EI refers to your ability to align with values of the greater good, which could be in your community (including virtual ones), workplace, or department.

❖ *Can you work for the group's good, putting them first?*

Communities and organizations rely on the commitment individuals make to the greater good. Those who contribute time and resources to ensure a positive impact experience greater personal fulfillment. They also often demonstrate a higher-than-average EI.

> *Are you socially active and concerned for the well-being of others?*

> *Do you identify with your organization, or do you compare yourself?*

> *Are you fulfilled in helping others?*

This can be a difficult balance if you want to please people and are geared toward caretaking. *Caring for the needs of others cannot take over your ability to care for yourself.* There must be balance.

What gets in the way:

- Focus on what's in it for me
- The need for control
- Disconnect from community values and goals
- Self-centered, "I don't have time to do that, let someone else do it."

☙ Your Stress Reaction. Be insistent in creating balance as you manage the demands and needs of others with your needs.

Overdone Social Responsibility

Excessive Social Responsibility tends to yield feedback that you are:

- A martyr is someone who consistently puts group needs before their own
- Subjective, meaning favoring one community or cause over another just as worthy
- Concerned with others at the expense of yourself
- Overly sensitive to others' needs

Relationship Fall out

Too much Social Responsibility disrupts relationships with too many commitments and loyalty to groups, setting up barriers to personal intimacy. Excessive Social Responsibility shows up with martyrdom; denying the personal relationship is one more act of self-sacrifice.

Leadership Fall out

Epitomizing the servant leader with excessive Social Responsibility, the tendency is to overplay their commitment and self-sacrifice, giving more than anyone else - suffering for the cause. This martyr leader leverages guilt, assuming this will motivate their followers.

Team and Organizational Expressions

Teams and Organizations with over-engaged Social Responsibility tend to rally around a cause, minimizing individual contributions and engaging in comparisons of how much one gives. This can create turnover in the group due to personal burnout.

Suggestions for Excessive Social Responsibility

Develop a deeper understanding of your value through strengths-based assessment and coaching.

PROBLEM-SOLVING

This is one of the EI dimensions essential to achieving outstanding results. Many leaders say that solving problems is all that leaders do. This is only part of the story; however, how you approach a problem will set the tone for your team's ability to solve it.

Here are four steps to problem-solving:

1. **Define the problem**. You must define the problem correctly.
2. **Define the alternatives**. It is essential to find various other options rather than letting pressure force you to select something prematurely.
3. **Evaluate the alternatives**. What are the pros and cons of each, and how will each one work out?
4. **Implement the solution.** Too often, leaders jump to a solution before the problem is defined and communicated. This makes it harder for staff to engage because they have been left out of this loop and need the information to connect the dots.

You want to know you have the right problem to solve and the correct definition to find the right solutions. The Mastermind program has a separate module for problem-solving and goes into more detail. I have included a few strategies here you can use.

1. **Drill down method**. This is where you break down a problem into smaller parts. Let's say you must solve the problem of Readmissions. First, you want to identify why pts are readmitted and then break down each into smaller parts. It helps to draw it out. Use this technique with brainstorming and involve your team in the process.

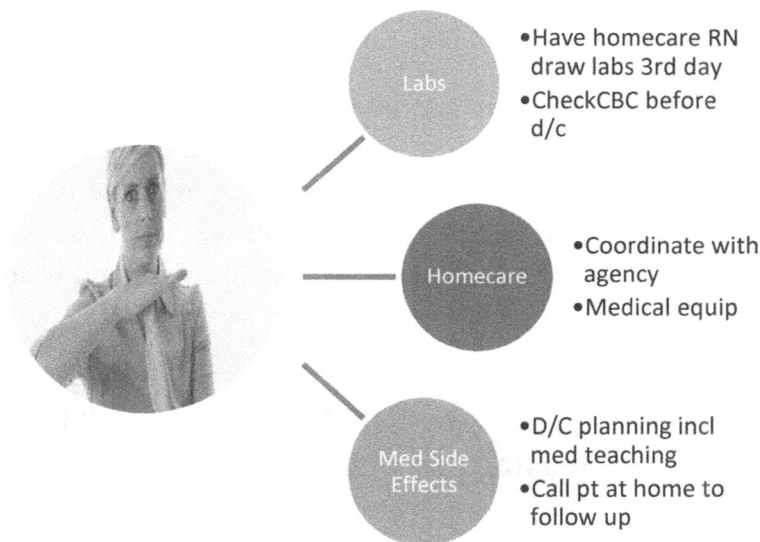

Labs
- Have homecare RN draw labs 3rd day
- CheckCBC before d/c

Homecare
- Coordinate with agency
- Medical equip

Med Side Effects
- D/C planning incl med teaching
- Call pt at home to follow up

2. **The 5 Why's.** Have you had a problem that keeps coming back? This process gives you an in-depth look at the problem from the people dealing with the issue rather than an educated guess by those in administration removed from the actual issue.

   This is a great way to look at a problem from where it is happening. It was developed in 1930 by the founder of Toyota and is still used today.

   Example: Staff will not comply with the new timecard protocol

   1. **Why?** They complain that they forget, and it is a new policy.

   2. **Why?** The policy was changed twice in the last year.

   3. **Why?** Management turnover.

   4. **Why?** The hospital lost accreditation, and people lost their jobs.

   5. **Why?** Lack of clear direction related to the overall organizational goals.

   Using the 5 Why's helps you get a broader look at the deeper issues. This scenario has a history of turnover, confusion, and needing action or communication about overall organizational goals. The staff acts "deaf" to directions from management and is not attentive. First, you need to get their attention and then communicate the new policy, why it is necessary, and what is in it for them.

   Use this process and talk to those directly involved to discover the 5 Why's.

   The 'Problem Solving' dimension is related to stress tolerance. It is easy to overlook problems and ideal solutions when stressed because of the false sense of urgency that is part of the stress reaction. As you learn to unhook from the stressful feelings using the many tools we provide in this training, you will earn the reputation of being capable and able to tackle challenging issues with fairness and wisdom.

&ent; Practice using the two methods to define the problem better. Reflect on and analyze what you learned in using this approach.

Overdone Problem Solving

Excessive Problem Solving tends to yield feedback that you:

- Engage problems too quickly without consideration of the root cause
- You may end up jumping into solving every conflict even though it is not your conflict to solve.

Relationship Fall out

Overdone problem-solving within a relationship creates a drive to confront every issue as a problem to solve. This comes at the expense of nurturing essential relationships.

Leadership Fall out

A leader with over-engaged Problem Solving tends to seek out problems and jump into them enthusiastically, even when reflection or delay may be the best approach. Leaders can appear aggressive, and followers can avoid interaction.

Team and Organizational Expressions

Teams or organizations with overdone Problem-solving tend to value confrontation, leading to interactions that can be insensitive. The ability to reflect and explore causes and issues compromises the quality of work produced.

Suggestions for Excessive Problem Solving

Consider the impact of jumping into the problem. How might this impact the entire group or the outcome? Do you have all the information you need? Engage your Flexibility to balance Problem-Solving.

Think through a chain of events logically. What is the likelihood that the worst-case scenario will happen? Engage Stress Tolerance to Balance Problem Solving.

REALITY TESTING

This impact training in emotional effectiveness is intended to help you develop greater self-awareness and insight into what you feel and how you see the world. Seeing the world through our mental models based on our experiences is human nature. Strengthening your emotional intelligence means that your view of "reality" may be skewed, based on your view of the world, while others will have their own model of reality or viewpoints.

It is essential to engage in active listening, ask questions, clarify any assumptions, and continue to operate based on facts (vs opinions and speculation). This requires discipline and objectivity.

Reality testing means that you operate based on the facts and not on how you want the world to be or think it "should" be.

Effective Reality Testing

- You take the time to find the facts and explore different points of view
- Know your assumptions and remove them from the process of evaluation
- Recognize your emotions can impact your conclusions
- Engage in strategies to reduce the stress reaction and release the potential of overreacting

What gets in the way:

- Lack of Self and other awareness
- Self-absorbed
- Fear, need to defend Self
- Need for status quo
- Overly stressed

∽ Are you objective as you consider the challenges/ opportunities that you face?

Overdone Reality Testing

Excessive Reality Testing tends to yield feedback that you are:

- Unimaginative
- Unable to trust your intuition or elements that are not verifiable facts
- Too objective, unable to consider the subjective, emotional aspects of the situation

Relationship Fall out

Overdone Reality Testing in a relationship compromises emotional exchange and understanding since everything is evaluated based on observable information. "I hear that you are sad, but you should not be." "You are angry, but it doesn't make sense to me that you are angry."

Leadership Fall out

In the extreme, Reality Testing prevents leaders from seeing the subjective aspects like emotional engagement and reading between the lines. Overdone Reality Testing can block a person's ability to project a future that cannot be seen, proven, or tangibly verified.

Team and Organizational Expressions

Teams or organizations that collectively overdo Reality Testing limit their vision of what is happening and block out more extensive possibilities for the future.

Suggestions for Excessive Reality Testing

Review the Ei dimensions of:

- Emotional Self-Awareness
- Optimism
- Flexibility
- Empathy

This will help you balance an overdone Reality Testing.

Impulse Control

Stanford did a longitudinal study many years ago called The Marshmallow Test. It tested a four-year-old's ability to resist eating a marshmallow. They were told that they would get another if they waited to eat the marshmallow until the next Interviewer arrived a short time later.

Twenty-five years later, the findings showed that those who could resist had much greater success in their life over the long term. This dimension of EI includes your ability to identify your reaction to a trigger and then take constructive action rather than reacting. You must know what triggers you, your typical reaction, and what would be a more effective response. You will develop greater impulse control as you activate resilience and build self-awareness.

It is helpful to anticipate your triggers and how you respond. List your triggers and your response.

Trigger	Response
1.	1.
2.	2.
3.	3.

What gets in the way:

- Too much stress and no strategy to manage it
- Lack of goals and objectives
- No self-awareness

Engage in the regular practice of mindfulness, gratitude breathing, and active listening. Improving this dimension will reap enormous dividends for you, including increased creativity.

Overdone Impulse Control

Excessive Impulse Control tends to yield feedback that you are:

- Unexpressive
- Emotionally detached
- Withdrawn or withholding in conversation
- Overly structured or planned

Relationship Fall out

Relationships suffer when a partner filters reactions, emotions, opinions, and needs so much that they become emotionally detached. This leaves their partner wondering what they think or feel and may lead to them second-guessing themselves.

Leadership Fall out

Leaders with excessive Impulse Control filter out how they feel, leaving followers to wonder. Effective leadership requires clear communication, including how the leader thinks and feels about issues.

Team and Organizational Expressions

Teams and organizations that overdo Impulse Control tend to engage less, sharing only what is necessary. Team members need the benefit of relationships to maintain the synergy and benefit of exceptional performance.

Suggestions for Excessive Impulse Control

Develop an Action Plan for your Ei; commit to at least two actions you will take to improve your skills in emotional intelligence and share your insights and developmental goals with at least one other person.

FLEXIBILITY

There is nothing as constant as change.

Flexibility is often misunderstood. Some people believe Flexibility is about going with the flow to avoid conflict. Sometimes, being flexible is because of a need for Assertiveness. We discussed Assertiveness earlier. Sometimes, leaders choose to be inflexible to demonstrate 'control' in the name of leadership.

Flexibility is your ability to adapt, shift, or adjust your behaviors, thoughts, and emotions to your requirements. At different times, leaders may stick to the plan just as it is appropriate to adapt or shift based on the new information.

Flexible people can change their minds about what is happening and adapt to the immediate demands. Every day, there are plenty of opportunities to be flexible. Small shifts may be required that may not have significant consequences, except they help nurture relationships and make it easy to get along, like choosing meeting dates and times or going to a different movie or restaurant. You may be required to learn new software or programs at work based on the job's demands. In most organizations, the changes are fast and furious from an administrative perspective and the demands of customers and stakeholders. Flexibility demands that you assess and evaluate the incoming information, adjust to meet your goals, and ensure the best possible outcomes.

The opposite of Flexibility is being overly attached to the familiar. Routine is a good thing. Rituals help conserve your energy and add a certain amount of order to the day. Whether driving the same way to work, eating the same lunch, or starting your day with meditation/ prayer, rituals can serve an excellent purpose to make life easier. And there are times when doing things how they have always been done gets in the way of success.

Being flexible is adjusting your reactions to have the best possible outcome.

A key to Flexibility is self-awareness. You can manage your emotions when you are aware of self-talk, stress triggers, or fears.

Next, an opportunity to reflect on your ability to be flexible...

Reflection:

The following will help you reflect on these concepts and develop your Flexibility. Write out responses.

Write out the routines or rituals that you have in the day:

i.e., Have coffee, check email, etc...

What happens when demands require you to vary these routines?

Has anyone suggested you need to be more flexible? In what way?

On a scale of 1-10, 10 being very flexible, how do you rate your ability to adjust?

| 0 | 1 | 2 | 3 | 4 | 5 | 6 | 7 | 8 | 9 | 10 |

On a scale of 1-10, 10 being high, how much do you insist on sticking to your routines?

| 0 | 1 | 2 | 3 | 4 | 5 | 6 | 7 | 8 | 9 | 10 |

Overdone Flexibility

Excessive Flexibility tends to yield feedback that you are:

- Prone to more starts than finishes
- Reluctant to stick to a plan and come to closure
- Unwilling or unable to make or keep personal commitments or even hold your ground
- Quickly bored with routine and predictability

Relationship Fall out

Excessive Flexibility can prove challenging in a personal relationship, showing up as a reluctance to commit to anything. Someone with too much Flexibility is always ready to start something new, and while exciting on one level, a relationship with this person will have more starts than finishes and very little predictability.

Leadership Fall out

Leaders who overdo Flexibility are so open to new data and experiences that their focus can change, compromising follow-through and consistency. It can be a challenge for followers to know what the leader considers necessary – now.

Team and Organizational Expressions

When Teams exhibit excessive Flexibility, the emphasis can be on reacting and changing with minor completion.

Suggestions for Excessive Flexibility

Set an attainable goal and move toward completion. Avoid setting the bar so high that you do not experience any positive feelings of achievement. Use Self Actualization to balance Flexibility. Self-actualization is more than achieving goals; it is also the ability to focus and finish goals without wavering.

RESILIENCE (STRESS TOLERANCE)

How well do you take a hit? Resilience is your ability to bounce back from challenges without permanent damage. Resilience is developed with a mind, body, and spirit strategy. It includes having enough energy to keep going when challenges show up, which means self-care is a part of the plan – enough sleep, the proper diet and exercise, meditation or mindfulness, and the pursuit of meaning.

Because of this program and the developed self-awareness, you will notice an increased ability to get through stressful times without being sidelined as a result of the hit. You will also learn strategies to build your resilience using both a heart-focused approach and mindfulness.

Activating your resilience regularly and daily will increase your capacity for stress and help you thrive where many people are stuck in the gridlock of time and demands.

What resilience looks like:

- Balance in lifestyle, choices, habits
- Ability to adapt
- Looks for the silver lining
- Self-care that includes a healthy diet, exercise, and lifestyle that supports the fulfillment of one's goals/ dreams/ aspirations

What gets in the way:

- Negative attitude
- Lack of goals
- Weak social network
- Blaming others

Check out the "Reflections" on the next page.

Reflection

How well do you take the hit?

Think about a time you recently bounced back. What made the difference in your ability to activate your resilience?

What is your self-talk when you are faced with a challenge?

Overdone Stress Tolerance

Excessive Stress Tolerance tends to yield feedback that you are:

- Blind to stressors and dangers that face you (You don't "get it")
- Emotionally disconnected
- Over-confident or conceited

Relationship Fall out

Excessive Stress Tolerance in a partner can come off as indifferent and unconcerned about the partner.

Leadership Fall out

Followers can interpret Excessive Stress Tolerance in a leader as not having to fear or take it very seriously. Leaders with this issue can lose credibility as followers must believe they accurately assess the situation.

Team and Organizational Expressions

Teams or organizations that collectively overdo Stress Tolerance tend to ignore any individual concerns of the members, decreasing the group's fellowship.

Suggestions for Excessive Stress Tolerance

The Ei dimensions that balance Stress Tolerance are:

- Emotional Self-Awareness
- Empathy
- Interpersonal Relationship
- Emotional Expression

Review these dimensions. Use Emotional Awareness to help you develop language around feelings.

OPTIMISM

Optimism is the ability to hold positive expectations and remain hopeful and resilient despite challenges. This is one of the characteristics of emotional intelligence that can be confusing.

Having a positive attitude means you believe in your ability to handle the challenge that shows up. It doesn't mean you ignore potential problems. Optimism is a combination of a hopeful attitude along with the ability to judge the situation realistically. This optimistic attitude results from believing in one's skills and abilities and recalling other times you successfully overcame this challenge.

Let's take a situation at work with Maria, one of the newer staff nurses:

> "The holiday schedule is coming out, and the manager has decided to have everyone draw straws for those who work on daydreaming the short straw and were assigned to work on the next holiday. Three of us were assigned. One of my coworkers complained bitterly that she always gets stuck during the holidays. Another coworker said, "Too bad I pulled the short straw, but at least I have the day after off, and I had off last year. My chances are good; I won't get the same draw next time." I did not say anything and reflected on the differences in attitude."

An optimistic attitude has three parts. Optimists see the situation as temporary and random instead of permanent and personal. "I always pick the short straw…" Optimists, "My chances are good not to get the short straw next time…"

Additionally, an optimistic attitude recognizes success will happen. Rather than, "I always get picked up, and I am sure next time will be the same way," the optimist says, "Chances are good next time, I will have time off."

"Why do bad things always happen to me," can be shifted to, "Even though I have to work the holiday, it could be slow, and I get called off. I had off last time."

While positive thinking is a part of being optimistic, it is not simply repeating positive affirmations. In our example, the optimist did not take having to work the holiday as a personal attack, permanent situation, or the overriding tone for her life.

✎ How can you increase your ability to be realistic and optimistic?

Reflection: Are You AN OPTIMIST or Pessimist?

Each question is going to help you make the distinction between an optimistic attitude and one that is pessimistic. If you have two or more "a" answers, you run the risk of a defeatist attitude. You could also be more damaging when stressed.

1) Bad things happen to me:
   a) Always
   b) Never
   c) Sometimes
2) My attitude is positive when:
   a) Pigs fly
   b) Something good happens
   c) Usually. I expect things to turn out.
3) When something terrible happens:
   a) I knew it would
   b) I get depressed
   c) There are always challenges. I can deal with it.
4) How would you describe yourself?
   a) Negative
   b) Critical
   c) Practical
5) How do others describe you?
   a) Negative
   b) Critical
   c) Practical

Overdone Optimism

Excessive Optimism tends to yield feedback that you are:

- Blind to reality and danger
- Biased toward opportunities that do not exist
- Let unrealistic belief in a positive outcome replace effort and hard work, which might otherwise have secured the positive result.

Relationship Fall out

Excessive Optimism in a relationship often comes across as a somewhat blind denial that problems exist, which can lead to disappointment and a crash later when the consequences of ignored behaviors appear.

Leadership Expression

The overly optimistic leader can come off as naïve and lacking credibility. This leader can discount followers who tend to bring up "negative" scenarios, seeing them as nay-sayers rather than contributors.

Team and Organizational Expressions

Teams and organizations with over-engaged Optimism tend to exude innocence and simplicity in which faithfulness is central, and complaints and doubts are not tolerated. This limits discussion, authentic problem-solving, and outcomes.

Suggestions for Excessive Optimism

The next time you find yourself with an overly optimistic vision of the future, consider the practical and objective facts. Use Reality Testing to balance your Optimism.

ABOUT THE AUTHOR

Dr. Cynthia Howard has worked with thousands of individuals, helping them break through barriers to their success. With over 22 years of experience as an Executive Coach and performance consultant, Dr. Howard uses her unique blend of experience as an entrepreneur and healthcare professional to transform businesses and employees into successful high performers.

During her graduate studies in psychology, Dr. Howard researched the impact of stress on performance. She recognized resilience skills and emotional intelligence as antidotes to the destructive influence of unchecked pressure. She uses Lean Six Sigma to define problems and explore solutions for organic engagement and outcome success.

Dr. Howard pioneered the Resilient Mindset and has developed a map to move leaders beyond burnout and complacency.

To contact Dr. Howard about this program, speak at your organization, or discover how this program can transform your leadership, email contact@worksmartclubnetwork.com.

ABOUT WORK SMART CONSULTING

Our mission is to support leaders and organizations who want to provide a workspace where people thrive. We are innovative, focused, and genius at unlocking potential and bringing out people's best.

We assess, coach, and train for high-performance building on the Lean Six Sigma process.

Contact us today and schedule a complimentary session to determine the best program for you and your workgroup.

Here is what one participant has said:

"I enjoyed having assessments, coaching, and training to help my team work better. I can see an improvement in how they come together and solve their problems. We now have tools to use to hold better meetings, manage communication, improve delegation, and so much more."

—Janice S., Director of Specialty Services

We help your leaders learn to think differently, value their time, and get more done consistently.

Please... STAY IN TOUCH

Stay connected to resources, webinars, and free tips on our social media sites.

Connect with us on Facebook:

www.facebook.com/worksmartclub

Connect with us on LinkedIn:

www.linkedin.com/in/drcynthiahoward

Subscribe to our YouTube channel

www.youtube.com/channel/worksmartclub